#17
Jefferson Branch Library
2211 W. Jefferson Boulevard
Los Angeles, CA 90018

LOOKING AT
COUNTRIES

Looking at the
CONGO

Kathleen Pohl

Reading consultant: Susan Nations, M.Ed.,
author/literacy coach/consultant in literacy development

Gareth Stevens
Publishing

Please visit our Web site at www.garethstevens.com.
For a free color catalog describing Gareth Stevens Publishing's list
of high-quality books, call 1-800-542-2595 (USA)
or 1-800-387-3178 (Canada). Gareth Stevens Publishing's fax: 1-877-542-2596

Library of Congress Cataloging-in-Publication Data

Pohl, Kathleen.
    Looking at the Congo / Kathleen Pohl.
      p. cm. — (Looking at countries)
    Includes bibliographical references and index.
    ISBN-10: 0-8368-8766-2   ISBN-13: 978-0-8368-8766-2 (lib. bdg.)
    ISBN-10: 0-8368-8773-5   ISBN-13: 978-0-8368-8773-0 (softcover)
    1. Congo (Democratic Republic)—Juvenile literature. I. Title.
  DT644.P64   2008
  967.51—dc22   2007039848

This edition first published in 2008 by
Gareth Stevens Publishing
A Weekly Reader® Company
1 Reader's Digest Road
Pleasantville, NY 10570-7000 USA

Senior Managing Editor: Lisa M. Guidone
Senior Editor: Barbara Bakowski
Creative Director: Lisa Donovan
Designer: Tammy West
Photo Researchers: Sylvia Ohlrich and Charlene Pinckney

Photo credits: (t=top, b=bottom, l=left, r=right)
Cover Per-Anders Pettersson/Getty Images; title page Martin Harvey, Gallo Images/Corbis;
p. 4 Marcus Wilson-Smith/Alamy; p. 6 Cyril Ruoso/JH Editorial/Minden Pictures; p. 7t Konrad
Wothe/Minden Pictures; p. 7b Bruce Davidson/Nature Picture Library; p. 8 De Agostini/Getty Images;
p. 9 Karl Ammann/Corbis (2); p. 10 Schalk Van Zuydam/AP Images; p. 11t Maurizio Gambarini/
Landov; p. 11b Euan Denholm/Reuters/Landov; p. 12 Eddie Gerald/Alamy; p. 13t Rodrique Ngowi/
AP Images; p. 13b Jacques Jangoux/Alamy; p. 14 Eddie Gerald/Alamy; p. 15t Sebastian Bolesch/
Das Fotoarchiv/Peter Arnold; p. 15b Martin Harvey, Gallo Images/Corbis; p. 16 Schalk Van Zuydam/
AP Images; p. 17t Nic Bothma/Corbis; p. 17b Robert Caputo/Aurora Photos; p. 18 Steve Turner/Alamy;
p. 19t Jacques Jangoux/Photo Researchers; p. 19b David Wall/Alamy; p. 20l Gary Cook/Alamy; p. 20r
Emilio Ereza/Alamy; p. 21 Mark Renders/Getty Images; p. 22 Nigel Cattlin/Photo Researchers; p. 23t
Jacky Naegelin/Landov; p. 23b AP Images; p. 24 Howard Burditt/Reuters/Landov; p. 25l Jose Azel/
Aurora Photos; p. 25r Michel Euler/AP Images; p. 26 Shutterstock; p. 27t Konrad Wothe/Minden Pictures;
p. 27b Per-Anders Pettersson/Getty Images

Printed in the United States of America

1 2 3 4 5 6 7 8 9 10 09 08 07

Contents

Words that appear in the glossary are printed in **boldface** type the first time they occur in the text.

Where Is the Congo?

The Congo is in central Africa. Its full name is the Democratic Republic of the Congo. The Congo has nine neighbors. To the west is the Republic of the Congo. The two names may sound almost the same, but the two countries are different. To the west, the Congo has a short coast on the Atlantic Ocean, too.

EUROPE

Atlantic Ocean

AFRICA

Indian Ocean

DEMOCRATIC REPUBLIC OF THE CONGO

The Democratic Republic of the Congo makes up much of central Africa.

Boats carry people and goods along the Congo River.

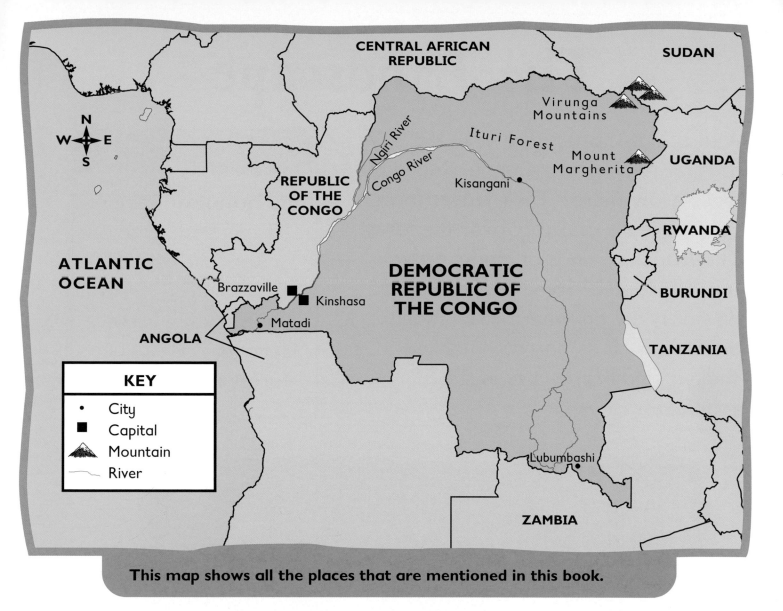

SUDAN

Virunga
Mountains

Ituri Forest

Ngiri River

Congo River

Mount
Margherita

UGANDA

Kisangani

REPUBLIC
OF THE
CONGO

RWANDA

ATLANTIC
OCEAN

DEMOCRATIC
REPUBLIC OF
THE CONGO

BURUNDI

Brazzaville

Kinshasa

Matadi

TANZANIA

ANGOLA

KEY

• City
■ Capital
▲ Mountain
〜 River

Lubumbashi

ZAMBIA

This map shows all the places that are mentioned in this book.

To the north are the Central African Republic and Sudan. Uganda, Rwanda, Burundi, and Tanzania border the Congo on the east. Zambia and Angola lie to the south.

Kinshasa is the capital and the country's biggest city. It has some tall, modern buildings and new homes. It also has some very poor areas with dirt roads.

The Congo River flows through much of the country. It is the fifth-longest river in the world and the second-longest river in Africa.

The Landscape

A thick **rain forest** grows in the northern half of the Congo. Many tall trees grow there. Their leaves form a roof, called a **canopy**, over the forest. Thousands of kinds of plants grow in the rain forest. Some of those plants do not grow anywhere else. Many animals, such as parrots, monkeys, snakes, and lizards, live in the rain forest.

Did you know?

The **bonobo** lives only in the Democratic Republic of the Congo. This great ape's home is the second-biggest rain forest in the world.

Bonobos, such as this young ape, live only in the rain forest south of the Congo River.

The Congo has **savannas** in the south. Those areas are grasslands with very few trees.

Mountains rise high in the east. Gorillas and baboons make their home there. Some of the mountains are volcanoes.

The Congo River flows through most of the country. It is an important waterway. People use boats to ship goods and to travel along the river.

This frog adds its call to the sounds of the rain forest.

The Virunga Mountains in the eastern Congo are a chain of volcanoes. The volcano shown here erupted, or blew up, in 2006.

Weather and Seasons

The climate in the Congo is **tropical**. It is very hot and wet most of the year. The hottest area is the rain forest. Thunderstorms are very common.

The savannas are cooler and drier. Sometimes rain does not fall for months. Animals such as lions, zebras, giraffes, and antelope live there.

A herd of buffalo graze on the dry savanna grasses.

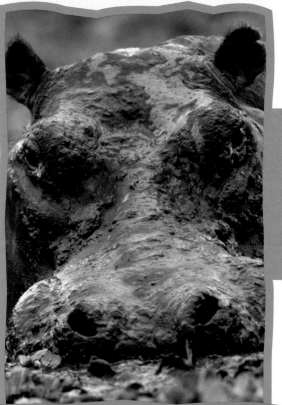

Mud keeps this hippo cool in a swamp in the Virunga National Park.

The sun rises over the rain forest. Many kinds of trees and other plants grow there.

In the east, breezes help keep the mountains cool. Temperatures can drop to freezing at night. Snow tops some of the mountains. Mount Margherita is the highest peak in the Congo.

Congolese People

More than sixty million people live in the Congo. Most live near the Congo River or in the highlands. One of three people is very poor. Some have no homes. People who have more money live in the cities or the **suburbs**. Suburbs are areas around the cities.

Most people in the Congo came from other parts of Africa long ago. Today, more than two hundred **ethnic groups** live in the Congo. Most groups have their own language. They have different ways of doing things. Sometimes the groups fight with each other. Fighting between groups within a country is called **civil war**.

Many Congolese women wear bright, colorful clothing. Some wear scarves on their heads.

These people are attending a church service. Half of the Congolese people are Roman Catholic.

A native woman rests after collecting firewood in the eastern Congo.

Half of the Congolese people are Roman Catholic. Others are Protestant. Some people follow African religions. A few are Muslim.

The official language of the Congo is French. It is spoken in schools and government offices. There are also four national languages and hundreds of local languages.

Country Life

Seven out of ten people live in the countryside. Most are farmers who can hardly feed their big families. Many people are very poor. Some do not have enough food to eat.

Farmers grow yams, which are like sweet potatoes. People also grow **cassava**, a root vegetable, and **plantains**, which are like bananas. Corn, rice, peanuts, and sugarcane are important crops. People in the country raise goats, sheep, cows, and pigs.

Women do most of the work in farm fields.

Fewer than half of the people in the Congo have clean drinking water. They must walk a long way to get water from a river.

These Congolese women collected firewood for cooking. They carry the wood on their heads.

Women usually work in the fields. They gather wood and cook over open fires. Most villages do not have electric lights or running water. Often, the water is not clean enough for drinking.

City Life

Some people come to the Congo's cities to look for work. Kinshasa is home to six million people. It has tall office buildings and art museums. It has a college and a big sports stadium, too.

Some people in Kinshasa have good jobs. Many others are very poor. The rich people live in a modern suburb. It has paved streets, electricity, and lights. Many other parts of the city do not.

Did you know?

Kinshasa lies across the Congo River from Brazzaville, the capital of the Republic of the Congo. The two cities are the closest country capitals in the world.

Kinshasa, shown here at night, is the capital of the Democratic Republic of the Congo.

This Congolese woman sweeps outside her shop in Kinshasa.

Matadi is the Congo's main port. It is halfway between Kinshasa and the Atlantic Ocean.

Lubumbashi is a big city in the south. It is in a part of the Congo that has many copper mines. Kisangani and Matadi are busy ports on the Congo River. Goods are shipped into and out of these ports.

Congolese Houses

In the cities, most apartments are made of cement blocks. In poor areas, people live in small houses made of mud bricks.

Some people in the Congo are **refugees**. They have left nearby countries that are at war. Refugees often live in tents in crowded camps.

Did you know?

Most villages in the Congo do not have phone lines. Many people, however, use cell phones.

People live in apartments in this thin building in Kinshasa. On the first floor are shops.

In the country, most people live in houses of dried mud and sticks. The **thatched** roofs are made of grass or palm leaves. People who have more money might live in a house with a metal roof. It catches the rainwater that runs off, so people can use it. Poor people must get water from a village pump or a river.

These women weave palm leaves to make a thatched roof.

This two-floor home is made of dried mud and has a thatched roof.

Congolese Food

Most people in the Congo eat only one or two meals a day. They eat a lot of starchy foods, such as corn, cassava, and rice. Cassava or rice is cooked and then served in a big bowl. People reach in with one hand and help themselves. They mix the rice or cassava with a spicy sauce. They shape the mixture into balls and eat it.

These women pound cassava roots to make flour. The flour is used to make cassava bread, which is eaten daily.

Congolese people grow and eat bananas. They also cook meat in "packets" made from banana leaves.

Bananas and plantains are important foods. They are eaten raw, fried, steamed, or mashed.

In the cities, restaurants serve spicy stews. They are made with vegetables and chicken or beef. Goat and catfish are on the menu, too.

Did you know?

People in the Congo do not have much money to buy meat. Sometimes they eat bats or grubs, the young of certain insects. Grubs look like worms.

At Work

Some people in the Congo grow crops to sell. They tap rubber trees for **latex**, a milky white liquid that is used to make rubber. To collect the latex, workers make cuts in the trees. People also grow palm trees for oil. Farmers grow and sell cotton and coffee, too.

The Congo is very rich in **natural resources**. Natural resources are materials that are supplied by nature, such as coal and wood. Much of the land in the Congo is covered with forests. People cut down trees for their wood, which is used to make furniture.

A rubber tree is tapped, and the latex is collected in a bowl.

A health care worker tests blood at a medical center.

Villagers pan for diamonds in a riverbed.

Mining is a main business in the Congo. People look for diamonds and copper in mines in the southeastern and eastern parts of the country. They also mine gold and a metal called **cobalt**. Cobalt is used to make magnets, jet engines, and colored glass.

In cities, people work in hotels, shops, and banks. They teach school and work in health clinics. Some people work in **factories**, too. They make tires, shoes, clothing, and cement.

Having Fun

Many people in the Congo like sports, especially soccer. They play it on the streets and at school. They watch their teams play at sports stadiums. Basketball and track and field are popular sports, too. People in the Congo and other parts of Africa like to play a board game called mancala.

Did you know?

Traditional Congolese dances celebrate big events in life, such as the birth of a child or a good growing season for crops.

Soccer has many fans among the Congolese people. Here, the Democratic Republic of the Congo's national team plays a match against South Africa.

Native people of the Ituri Forest dance to celebrate important events.

A Congolese man returns the ball during a game of tennis in Kinshasa.

Music and dance are a big part of life in the Congo. People in villages play wooden flutes and beat on drums. They dance and sing. In the cities, especially Kinshasa, many people enjoy dancing at nightclubs. Jazz music is popular, too.

Christmas and Easter are the main religious holidays. People observe New Year's Day and Independence Day, too. A special holiday is Parents' Day. On that day, August 1, families go to cemeteries. They honor the dead by cleaning their graves. Then the families have a picnic.

The Congo: The Facts

• The Democratic Republic of the Congo was renamed in 1997. Before then, the country was called Zaire (zah-EER).

• The Congo used to be ruled by Belgium, a country in Europe. In 1960, the Congo became independent, or free from outside control.

• In the past, the Congo has not been a true **democracy**. The people did not elect their leaders. Instead, one leader, a **dictator**, was the head of the country. Since 1990, the Congo's government has slowly given its people more freedom. Recently, the people voted for a president. The president is head of the government.

• The Congo is a country of unrest. At times, its people are at war with one another and with the country's neighbors.

The flag of the Democratic Republic of the Congo has a blue background. The color blue stands for peace. A yellow star in the corner stands for the hope of a bright future.

Okapis are related to giraffes. Okapis use their long, dark tongues to grasp leaves — and to clean their eyes and ears!

The Congo's unit of money is the Congolese franc. Franc paper notes have different pictures on them.

Glossary

ancestors – family members who lived in the past

bonobo – a kind of great ape, similar to the chimpanzee

canopy – the top layer of branches and leaves that covers a rain forest

cassava – a starchy root vegetable

civil war – a war in which people in the same country fight each other

cobalt – a metal that is used to make products such as magnets, jet engines, and colored glass

continent – a large landmass

democracy – a government in which the people elect their leaders

dictator – one leader who rules a country in which the people have no power

ethnic groups – groups of people with the same cultures, traditions, and ways of life

factories – buildings where goods are made

latex – a milky white liquid used to make rubber

natural resources – resources supplied by nature, such as forests, rivers, and minerals, that people use for industry

okapi – a plant-eating animal similar to a giraffe

plantains – banana-like fruits that grow in tropical places

rain forest – a very thick forest in a tropical climate where tall trees form a canopy

refugees – people who flee their country, often for political or religious reasons

savannas – areas of grasslands with few trees

suburbs – areas that are outside a city

thatched – made of bundles of grass, palm leaves, or straw

tropical – very hot and damp

Find Out More

All About Nature
www.allaboutnature.com/subjects/apes

National Geographic
www.nationalgeographic.com/congotrek360

Teach the Children
www.teachthechildrenwell.com/social.html

Zoom School
www.zoomschool.com/school/Africa

Publisher's note to educators and parents: Our editors have carefully reviewed these Web sites to ensure that they are suitable for children. Many Web sites change frequently, however, and we cannot guarantee that a site's future contents will continue to meet our high standards of quality and educational value. Be advised that children should be closely supervised whenever they access the Internet.

My Map of the Congo

Photocopy or trace the map on page 31. Then write in the names of the countries, bodies of water, cities, provinces, and territories listed below. (Look at the map on page 5 if you need help.)

After you have written in the names of all the places, find some crayons and color the map!

Countries
Angola
Burundi
Central African Republic
Democratic Republic of
   the Congo
Republic of the Congo
Rwanda
Sudan
Tanzania
Uganda
Zambia

Bodies of Water
Atlantic Ocean
Congo River
Ngiri River

Cities
Brazzaville (Republic of
   the Congo)
Kinshasa
Kisangani
Lubumbashi
Matadi

Land Areas and Mountains
Ituri Forest
Mount Margherita
Virunga Mountains

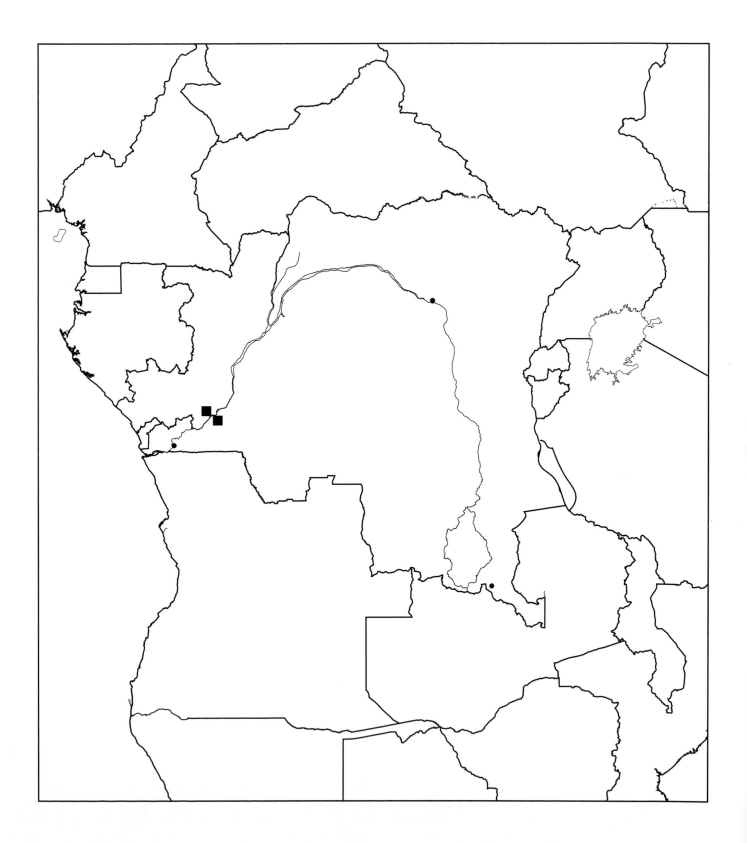

Index